We Take Our Turns

Remember to store up an accurate
remembrance of the way
in which God comforts thee.
F.B. Meyer

cover art and illustrations
by Shay Boomer

**When we get together,
I want to encourage you in your faith,
but I also want to be encouraged by yours.**

Romans 1:12 NLT

Encourage: to receive solace
and encouragement in the
society of others

Introduction

One morning I woke up with the idea to
assemble a small book from my journals—
inspired by times of trial and loss,
when my attention span was meager.
These were times when God so lovingly broke
His daily bread into bite size pieces, knowing what
was needed for the hours ahead.

The name "We Take Our Turns" came to mind,
as we all take our turns in the mountains and valleys.
The other spin on "We Take Our Turns" is to pass
the book along when you are finished. Maybe write
a note or two if you like, and let it travel around
from friend to friend.

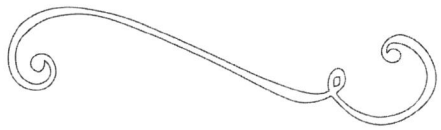

I wrote some of these journal entries while I was writing and recording
Scripture Songs Volume One and
Scripture Songs Volume Two—
which is why certain verses have song titles.

For over twenty years I've been writing songs,
recording, speaking and traveling.
The stage never pulled me onto all those
airplanes. (I'm an introvert, mostly).
It's people like you, the stories we share,
and the faith we tend to in each other.

I hope you find a word or two,
just for you.

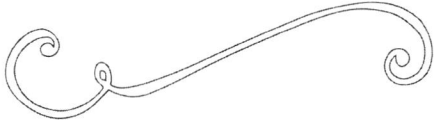

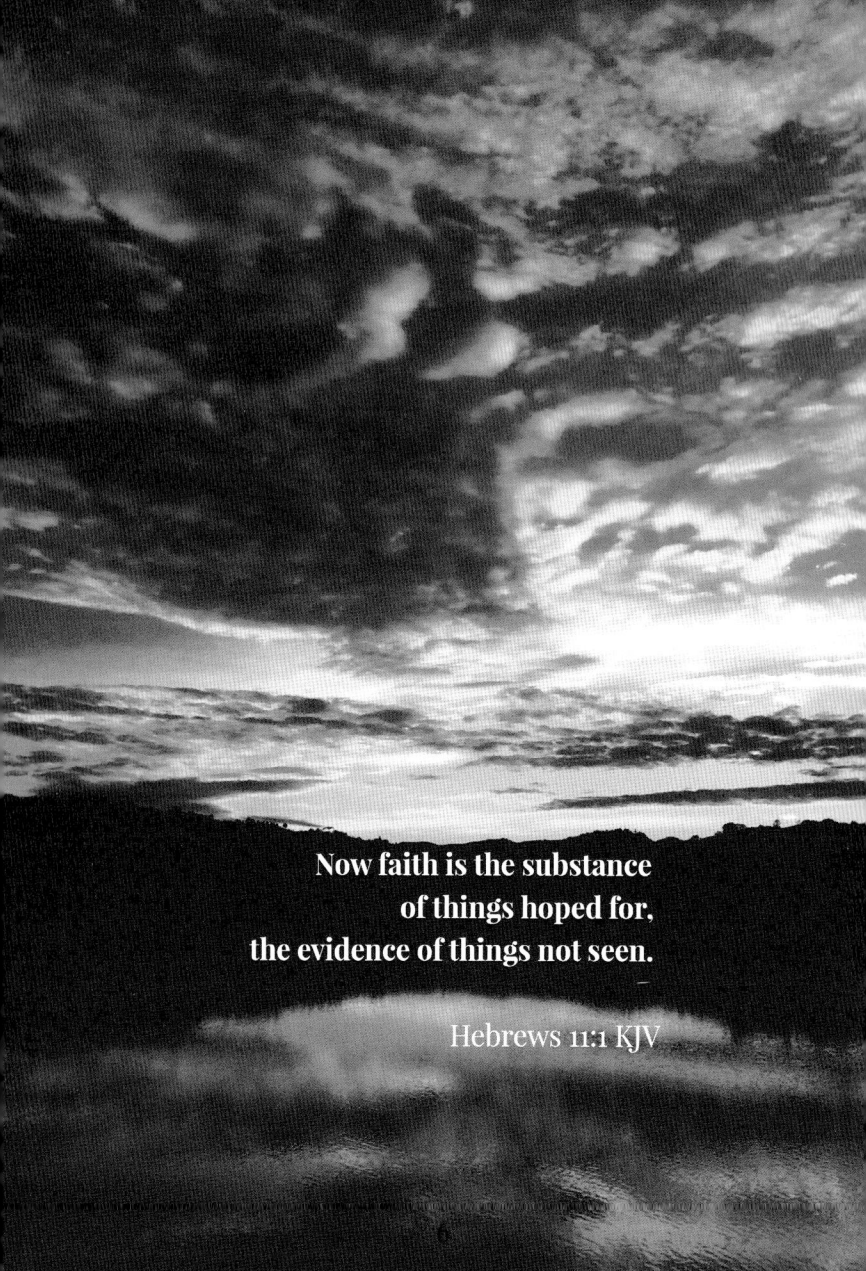

Now faith is the substance
of things hoped for,
the evidence of things not seen.

Hebrews 11:1 KJV

Evidence of things not seen.

Like breadcrumbs along the path.
Thoughts, words, memories,
generated outside my human mind.

My part is to search,
especially when I don't see or feel.

Search until the unseen
gains more ground than the seen.

Like shaking off a nightmare as a child.
Waiting for life awake to eclipse
the lingering dream.

Your words hold my trembling hands
until assurance comes.

In this you greatly rejoice,
though now for a little while,
if need be,
you have been grieved
by various trials,
that the genuineness of your
faith, being much more
precious than gold
that perishes,
though it is tested by fire,
may be found to
praise, honor, and glory
at the revelation of
Jesus Christ,
whom having not seen
you love.

1 Peter 1:6–8a NKJV

A Sparkle in the Mud

Faith is much more precious than gold.
So dig and sweat and never lose hope.

When it appears everyone else
is striking it rich,
but all you see is dirt,
still search.

Every day.

Like panning for gold:
as water swirls over dirt,
a fleck appears.

A flash of His presence.

A sparkle in the mud.

And a wealth of miraculous peace
overshadows all earthly everything.

...you have been grieved by various trials,

1 Peter 1:6–8 NKJV

In the middle of trials,
especially those of health and mind,
condemnation creeps in.

The undercurrent lie is God likes us
best running at full strength
(which is pretty much never for me).

The truth is,
some of the sweetest worship filling heaven
is whispered from hospital beds.

And sometimes the most valiant act of faith
is simply standing still.

Be still, and know that I am God.

Psalm 46:10 ESV

**But He said to them,
"Where is your faith?"**

Luke 8:25 NKJV

Things spinning in my mind. 3 a.m. and feeling alone. Future. Bank account. Health. Where is my faith? Brush this question over each anxious thought, one by one— the ongoing trial and remedy, the cultivation of faith— misplaced and then re-placed back where it belongs.

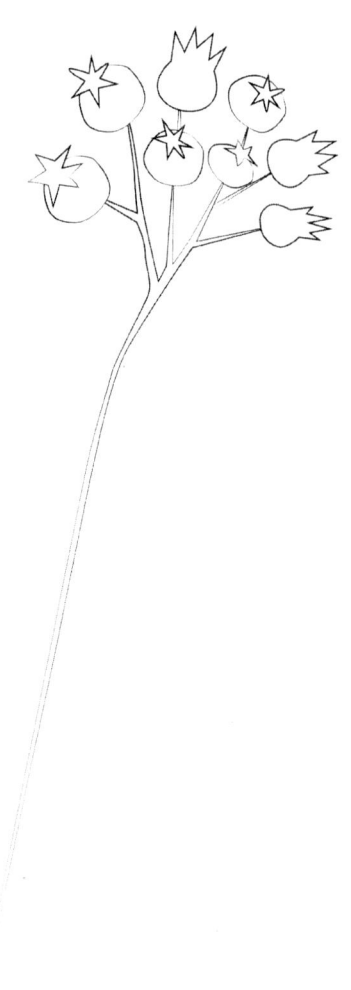

No faith is so precious
as that which lives and triumphs
through adversity.

Tested faith brings experience.

You would never have believed
your own weakness
had you not needed to pass
through trials.

And you would never have known
God's strength
had His strength not been needed
to carry you through.

C.H. Spurgeon

While on earth,
we have the unique opportunity
to love Him before we see Him.

Angels don't even get this chance.

**...whom having not seen you love.
Though now you do not see Him,
yet believing,
you rejoice with joy inexpressible
and full of glory**

1 Peter 1:8 NKJV

The most important moment in my life

is seeing Jesus face to face.

Maybe all life works backwards

from that one moment.

 I won't ever regret any faith-forging fire.

He does not delight
in the strength of the horse;
He takes no pleasure
in the legs of a man.
The Lord takes pleasure
in those who fear Him,
In those who hope in His mercy.

Psalm 147:10-11 NKJV

Through a run of sleepless nights and pounding thoughts, this verse gives me something to hold. Beyond my helplessness, even if I find no relief–in any state– I can hope in his mercy;

God has only been merciful to me.

Faith trusts He stays the same—
even when life *doesn't.*

All Who Are Weary

Six Inches of Sky

"Come to me,
all you who are weary
and burdened,
and I will give you rest.

Take my yoke upon you
and learn from me,
for I am gentle
and humble in heart,
and you will find rest
for your souls."

Matthew 11:28–29 NIV

It's one thing for me to see
the beauty in these words
(and I do, every time).

It's a whole other thing
to accept the invitation.

Three times I pleaded
with the Lord about this,
that it should leave me.

But he said to me,

"My grace is sufficient for you,
for my power is made perfect
in weakness."

Therefore I will boast
all the more gladly
of my weaknesses,

so that the power of Christ
may rest upon me.

2 Corinthians 12:8-9 ESV

For the sake of Christ, then,
I am content with

weaknesses,

insults,

hardships,

persecutions,

and calamities.

For when I am weak,
then I am strong.

2 Corinthians 12:10 ESV

God is the Strength of My Heart
Scripture Songs Volume 2

**Whom have I in heaven but You?
And there is none upon earth
that I desire besides You.**

**My flesh and my heart fail;
But God is the strength of my heart
and my portion forever.**

Psalm 73:25–26 NKJV

A lot of Bible versions read,
"My flesh and my heart *may* fail."
I chose to record the
New King James Version
because it doesn't leave the option.

Portion: something allotted to
or belonging to a person—
something set aside just for you.

God is my portion forever.

I always have Him to look forward to.

For God, who said,

"Let there be light in the darkness,"

has made this light shine in our hearts

so we could know the glory of God

that is seen in the face of Jesus Christ.

2 Corinthians 4:6 NLT

I think of His eyes

When I think of His earthly face,
I think of His eyes.

His eyes looking through outward things
to inward things.

I think of mercy drawing His eyes
toward the weakest and sickest.

Toward anyone with a shred of faith,
or even the possibility of faith.

All I had was emptiness
the day I discovered His attention.

He had seen me all along.

What He doesn't see is also profound

"...and I will remember their sins no more."

Hebrews 8:12 ESV

...as far as the east is from the west,
so far does he remove our transgressions
from us.

Psalm 103:12 ESV

But as He went,
the multitudes thronged Him.
Now a woman,
having a flow of blood for twelve years,
who had spent all her livelihood on physicians
and could not be healed by any,
came from behind
and touched the border of His garment.

And immediately her flow of blood stopped.

And Jesus said,
"Who touched Me?"
When all denied it,
Peter and those with him said,
"Master, the multitudes
throng and press You,
and You say,
'Who touched Me?'"

Luke 8:43-45 NKJV

Jesus sees differently

The disciples stood next to Him

and only saw the crowd,

the impossible.

But Jesus said,
"Somebody touched Me,
for I perceived power
going out from Me."
Now when the woman saw
that she was not hidden,
she came trembling;
and falling down before Him,

she declared to Him
in the presence of all the people
the reason she had touched Him
and how she was healed immediately.

And He said to her,
"Daughter, be of good cheer;
your faith has made you well.
Go in peace."

Luke 8:46-48 NKJV

He felt a frightened woman
come from behind and touch
the edge of His clothes.
He stopped and called
until her eyes met His.

Then Jesus gave her
what she didn't know she needed—

He healed her image of God.

Jesus taught her
the true expression on God's face,
and the true tone of God's voice.

I wonder,

as she went home,

if she smiled bigger

from her physical healing

or because Jesus

called her daughter

and noticed her faith?

I think I know.

One moment with Jesus

and she had a new story of her life—

a new story to tell.

He is the image of the invisible God...

Colossians 1:15 ESV

I know now, Lord,

why You utter no answer.

You are Yourself the answer.

Before Your face questions die away.

What other answer would suffice?

C.S. Lewis

I can't remember where I found this quote.

But I do remember it inspired the song—

"Draw Me Near" from the album,

These Things Don't Change.

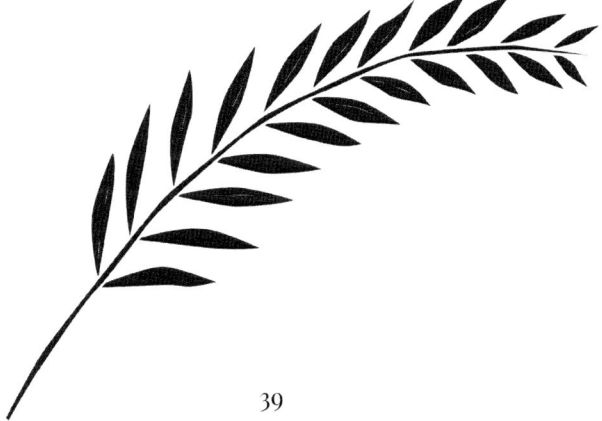

Paul prayed in Ephesians 1:17
—that they would have a revelation of Jesus.

When isn't this a good prayer to pray?

For my friend,

   for my enemy,

      for my family,

         for the lost,

for the struggling,

   for the teacher,

      for the pastor,

         for the sick,

            for the student,

      for myself.

Revelation:

something revealed or disclosed,

especially a striking disclosure,

as of something not yet realized.

They couldn't bring him to Jesus
because of the crowd,
so they dug a hole through the roof
above his head.
Then they lowered the man on his mat,
right down in front of Jesus.

Mark 2:4 NLT

Everything is right in His presence

It's worth every second of time,

every drop of sweat,

and every push through the crowd

to bring those we love to Jesus.

And when there is no roof to dig through,

we can bring our friends to Him in prayer.

Right down in front of Him,

day or night—

from anywhere in the world.

And above all things
have fervent love for one another,
for "love will cover a multitude of sins."

1 Peter 4:8 NKJV

Love covers

We all see faults in each other.
Especially those we know well.
Like bark on a tree,
love covers and protects vulnerable places.

Love is patient.

    Love is kind.

        Love bears all things,

            believes all things,

                hopes all things,

                    endures all things,

Love Never Fails
Scripture Songs Volume One

If I speak with the tongues
of men and of angels, but do not have love,
I have become a noisy gong or a clanging cymbal.
If I have the gift of prophecy,
and know all mysteries and all knowledge;
and if I have all faith,
so as to remove mountains,
but do not have love, I am nothing.
And if I give all my possessions to feed the poor,
and if I surrender my body to be burned,
but do not have love, it profits me nothing.
Love is patient, love is kind
and is not jealous;
love does not brag and is not arrogant,
does not act unbecomingly;
it does not seek its own, is not provoked,
does not take into account a wrong suffered,
does not rejoice in unrighteousness,
but rejoices with the truth; bears all things,
believes all things, hopes all things, endures all things.

Love never fails...

1 Corinthians 13:4-8 NASB

People fail though.
Even with best intentions.

If insecurity and heartache
overstay their visit,
carefully inspect your heart,
and see if humans are crowding
the space meant only for God.

I've been crushed on both sides
of the impossible weight
of misplaced expectations.

I think we all have scars.

He can use those too.

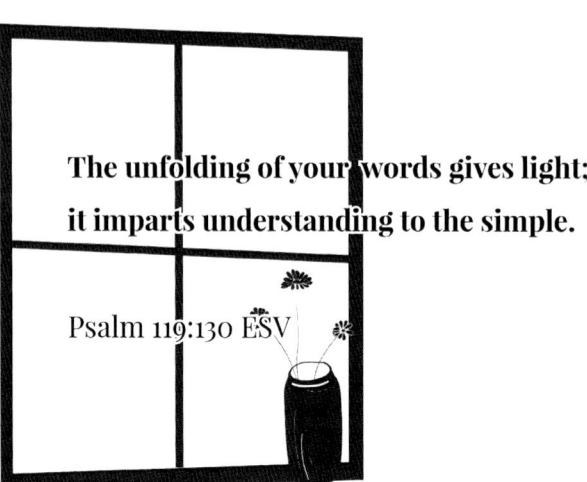

The unfolding of your words gives light;
it imparts understanding to the simple.

Psalm 119:130 ESV

Like embers falling
from heaven,
God touches the simple
with His brilliance.

It's work to maintain
a dark room in daylight.
Especially with windows
and doors inviting entrance.
The slight fold of a drape bleeds
enough light to break sleep.

(I know this from late night hotel arrivals—
hoping to hold off the morning).

Sometimes I stare at His words
like a thick curtain closed,
when right behind is a blazing sun.

We now have this light
shining in our hearts,
but we ourselves
are like fragile clay jars
containing this great treasure.

This makes it clear
that our great power
is from God,
not from ourselves.

2 Corinthians 4:7 NLT

Some of the greatest treasure on earth
is found in the most fragile of jars.

... Although the doors were locked, Jesus came and stood among them and said, "Peace be with you."

John 20:26 ESV

When others mourn
and words cannot be found.
Remember Jesus walks effortlessly
through locked doors.

Prayer travels where words cannot.

I think of all the times Jesus brought peace
into my impossible places.

Places where words couldn't travel
and hands couldn't be held.

Standing at my mom's bedside in ICU—
my sister next to me.

Standing in the center of our worst fear.

With voice frail and choked, my sister says,
"I have peace."

I whisper back, "I do too.
I don't know what it means, but I do too."

We didn't know if mom's personality
would come back to her eyes.

What we did know was Jesus stood with us
and His presence brought peace.

Impossible, miraculous,
breathtaking peace.

I don't think I have thanked Him
enough for that moment.

Or a million other moments.

Thanking Him now ♡

**Surely goodness and mercy shall follow me
all the days of my life...**

Psalm 23:6 NKJV

Follow: to run after

hunt

pursue

Every day of life,

yesterday,

tomorrow,

forever,

and right this minute,

God's goodness and mercy pursue us.

The steadfast love
of the Lord
never ceases;
his mercies never
come to an end;
they are new
every morning;
great is your faithfulness.
"The Lord is my portion,"
says my soul,
"therefore I will hope in him."

Lamentations 3:22–24 ESV

We are surrounded by mercies:

Behind,

before,

and they never

come to an end.

All the days of our lives.

For this reason I bow my knees before the Father...

Ephesians 3:14 ESV

Paul in chains—

people locked out—

feet helpless to go—

hands helpless to fix—

Only God can hear.

Only God can answer.

On his knees, Paul was free.

And when the Pharisees saw this,
they said to his disciples,
"Why does your teacher
eat with tax collectors
and sinners?"

But when he heard it, he said,
"Those who are well
have no need of a physician,
but those who are sick.

Go and learn what this means:
'I desire mercy, and not sacrifice.'
For I came not to call the righteous,
but sinners."

Matthew 9:11–13 ESV

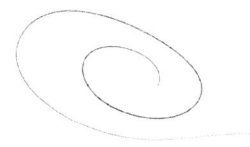

At the hairdresser

My hair is wrapped in foil
and I'm listening to conversations
about a celebrity.
They say he has blond hair
and an anger problem.

This morning I read Jesus ate with sinners.
It is not the healthy who need a doctor.
He came for the sick.
He came for everyone I see right now—

including the one in the mirror.

Flying to Seattle

**Then He lifted up His eyes
toward His disciples, and said:**

**Blessed are you poor,
for yours is the kingdom of God.**

**Blessed are you who hunger now,
for you shall be filled.**

**Blessed are you who weep now,
for you shall laugh.**

Luke 6:20-21 ESV

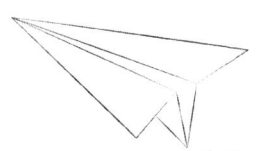

Jesus still turns
His eyes toward us

Blessed are you poor—

poor: needing, wanting, out of things,
helpless, powerless to accomplish an end

**But he said to me,
"My grace is sufficient for you,
for my power is made perfect
in weakness."**

2 Corinthians 12:9 ESV

A gentle moment
in the midst of Alzheimers

I'm remembering dad watching TV
with his drug store reading glasses.
I told him they were for reading.
He smiled, nestled in, and said,
"I know.
I'm just trying something different—
something new."

Retreat notes

Theme: Everlasting Father
Speaker (and friend) Sandy MacIntosh

"Father speaks to the lonely part of me,

the frightened part,

the child.

Here we can rest.

It does us well to realize

we are children of our Heavenly Father."

**Anxiety in the heart of a man causes depression,
but a good word makes it glad.**

Proverbs 12:25 NKJV

search and pray for good words—
then give them away...

text,

call,

write...

The Lord is near to the brokenhearted and saves the crushed in spirit. Psalm 34:18

A GOOD WORD

A GOOD WORD

If I take the wings of the morning and dwell in the uttermost parts of the sea, even there your hand shall lead me, and your right hand shall hold me. Psalm 139:9-10 ESV

In the Shelter
Scripture Songs Volume 2

**Hear my cry O God,
attend to my prayer,
from the end of the earth
I will cry to You.**

**When my heart is overwhelmed,
lead me to the Rock
that is higher than I.**

**For You have been a shelter for me,
A strong tower from the enemy.
I will abide in Your tabernacle forever;
I will trust in the shelter of Your wings.**

Psalm 61:1-2 NKJV

I recorded this song
two weeks after losing Dad.
All the Psalms on this record
were like the hands I held
during that time.

Overwhelm: bury or drown
beneath a huge mass

Mourning feels like drowning.
Every trace of energy
fights to find the surface
and breathe without effort.

Then another wave crashes,
and another.

My flesh fails to save me.
I cry for deliverance.
I cry for the shore
and another wave crashes.

I never knew mourning
would take such faith.

**...I will trust
in the shelter of Your wings.**

Psalm 61:4 NKJV

Clinging to David's words— like a lifesaver.
The kind of lifesaver you float on while waiting for
rescue.

I would have lost heart, unless I had believed

That I would see the goodness of the Lord in the land of the living

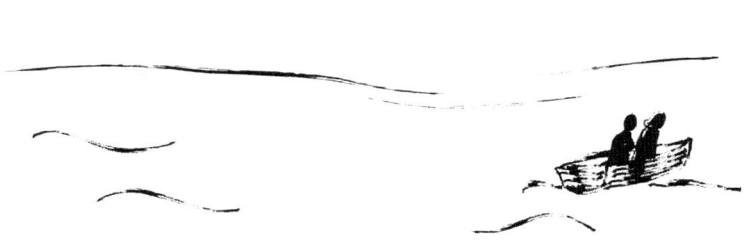

Wait on the Lord: Be of good courage
And He shall strengthen your heart Psalm 27:13-14

I lie awake thinking of you,
meditating on you
through the night.

I think of how much
you have helped me;
I sing for joy
in the shadow
of your protecting wings.

Psalm 63:6-7 NLT

Listen, my beloved brethren:
did not God choose
the poor of this world
to be rich in faith
and heirs of the kingdom
which He promised
to those who love Him?

James 2:5 ESV

Faith is the rich treasure
in the heart of the penniless.

Then Jesus said to him,
"Put your sword back into its place.
For all who take the sword
will perish by the sword.

Do you think that I cannot
appeal to my Father,
and he will at once
send me more
than twelve legions of angels?

But how then should
the Scriptures be fulfilled,
that it must be so?"

Matthew 26:52–54 ESV

The laser focus of Jesus

One angel could have easily done the job.
A legion equaled 6000 troops
12 X 6000 = 72,000

More spectacular than
the thousands of angels
ready to burst through the sky
instantly,
was His resolve to say no.

Scripture was the path He chose,
writing our new life with every step.

**...For we have no power
to face this vast army that is attacking us.
We do not know what to do,
but our eyes are on You.**

2 Chronicles 20:12 NIV

He counts the number of the stars
and calls them all by name.

Psalm 147:4

And I pray
that Christ will be
more and more
at home in your hearts,
living within you
as you trust in him.
May your roots
go down deep
into the soil of God's
marvelous love;

Ephesians 3:17 TLB

at home: welcome, invited,
free to be yourself
opposite: unwelcome, uninvited,
unaccepted

Be fully at home in my heart.

Trust in the Lord
with all your heart,
and do not lean
on your own
understanding.
In all your ways
acknowledge him,
and he will
make straight your paths.

Proverbs 3:5–6 ESV

I don't realize I'm leaning too hard on a thing until it fails and I fall with it

Today I got news
I wasn't expecting (lab results)
and it knocked the wind right out of me.

I read this verse in the morning
and hoping for a little medicine,
I revisited it in the evening.

Acknowledge means to recognize
and know:
In all my ways recognize and know Him.
When I slip from recognizing
and knowing Him,
discontent and fear infiltrate.

The straight path
is the one leading
straight to Him.

Nothing was easy
about the path
Jesus walked.

He is both the destination
and the comfort along the way

He isn't always in the quick rescue.

Instead, like the deepest of friends,

He gets soaked in the storm with you.

A friend loves at all times.

Proverbs 17:17 ESV

Somewhere in Ohio
Pieces of stories I hear –

"Been a long time since
I had natural pineapple –
'bout 4 years maybe,
I've just had the kind
in the can."

"That girl with the bad knee
might need two or three
more surgeries.
She chased a thief out
of her store and
his girlfriend ran her over."

It's midnight —
not sure what town I'm in.
There is no service —
can't text or call.

Then He spoke a parable
to them,
that men always ought
to pray
and not lose heart —
Luke 18:1

Condemnation invades like a thief.

It hides in the shadows
and steals and steals
as long as it stays undetected.

It keeps us miserable and isolated.
Like a low-grade fever,
it doesn't take us all the way down.

Condemnation tricks us into thinking
the remedy has to do with us.

**Therefore, since we have been justified
by faith, we have peace with God
through our Lord Jesus Christ.**
Romans 5:1 ESV

**There is therefore now no condemnation
for those who are in Christ Jesus.**
Romans 8:1 ESV

**What then shall we say to these things?
If God is for us, who can be against us?**
Romans 8:31 ESV

**For by grace you have been saved
through faith.
And this is not your own doing;
it is the gift of God,
not a result of works,
so that no one may boast.**
Ephesians 2:8–9 ESV

For I am sure
that neither death nor life,
nor angels nor rulers,
nor things present,
nor things to come,
nor powers,
nor height nor depth,
nor anything else in all creation,
will be able to separate us
from the love of God
in Christ Jesus our Lord.

Romans 8:38-39 ESV

Sure: confident in what one thinks or knows;
having no doubt that one is right

Jesus prayed—

"...that the love with which You loved Me may be in them, and I in them."

John 17:26b NKJV

Abandonment
threats, torment
bruises, blood
nothing on earth

ever

obscured Jesus'
good image
of His Father.

**When he was reviled,
he did not revile in return;
when he suffered,
he did not threaten,
but continued entrusting himself
to him who judges justly.**

1 Peter 2:23 ESV

And may you have
the power to understand,
as all God's people should,

how wide,

how long,

how high,

and how deep

his love is.

May you experience the love of Christ,
though it is too great to understand fully.
Then you will be made complete
with all the fullness of life and power
that comes from God.

Ephesians 3:18-19 NLT

I have prayed for you too—
for the power to understand
such a love as this.

To trust His heart at every turn.

All the way to the day
when every tear will be wiped away.

Heaven
Scripture Songs Volume One

**"... And God will wipe away
every tear from their eyes;
there shall be no more death,
nor sorrow, nor crying.
There shall be no more pain,
for the former things
have passed away."**

Revelation 21:4 NKJV

(This is my favorite song on the album).

I think I look forward to watching
other's tears brushed away by Jesus—
more than anything.

all will be made right at that moment

YOUR TURN